How To Be A Train Driver

And Everything Else About Trains

By Phil Jay

1: What Does A Train Driver Do?

All aboard! Welcome to the exciting world of trains! If you've ever watched a train zip by on the tracks or felt the rumble beneath your feet as it whooshed past, then you know just how magical these metal giants can be. But did you know that the person who sits at the very front of the train has one of the most exciting jobs in the world? That person is the train driver, and throughout this book, we're going to find out what a train driver really does!

The Captain of the Rails

A train driver is kind of like the captain of a ship or the pilot of an airplane, except instead of water or sky, they navigate long metal tracks that crisscross through cities, forests, mountains, and plains. Each morning, a train driver puts on their special uniform, grabs their schedule, and steps into the "cab"—the driver's seat at the front of the train. The cab is their own special office, filled with all sorts of buttons, levers, screens, and switches. From this seat, they are in total control of the train, guiding it forward, stopping at stations, and making sure every passenger or piece of cargo arrives safely at its destination.

Meet the Controls: The Train Driver's Toolbox

Once inside the cab, the train driver checks the control panel. This panel is like a giant game controller, with each button and lever having a very special job. The most important levers include:

The Throttle: This is what makes the train go faster or slower. Push it forward, and the train starts to pick up speed; pull it back, and it gently slows down. The Brake: Every train driver's best friend! This big, sturdy lever is what helps the train come to a complete stop. But stopping a train is a little trickier than stopping a car. Because trains are so heavy, they need plenty of time to slow down—sometimes as much as a mile before they reach the station! The Horn: With the press of a button, the train driver can make the train's horn blare loudly. This is a super important tool because it lets people nearby know the train is coming. The horn is also used to say a friendly "hello!" to anyone on the tracks. The Speedometer: Just like in a car, the train's speedometer tells the driver how fast they're going. Some trains can reach speeds of up to 200 miles per hour!

The Big Responsibility: Keeping Everyone Safe

Safety is a train driver's number 1 job. Every single day, drivers have to stay alert, pay attention to the signals, and be ready to react in a split second. When they see a green signal, they know the track ahead is clear, and it's safe to keep going. A yellow light means "slow down and be cautious," while a red light means "stop and wait." Signals are like a train's secret language, helping drivers navigate the tracks without crashing into each other.

Train drivers are also always in contact with a person called the Train Dispatcher, who watches over all the trains from a control centre. The dispatcher can tell them if there's a delay ahead, a storm, or even an animal on the tracks. With a good dispatcher and clear signals, the train driver can focus on guiding the train smoothly to its destination.

Meeting Passengers and Making Stops

One of the best parts of a train driver's day is seeing the passengers safely on board, ready to go on their adventures. Imagine looking out the window and seeing kids excited for a holiday, friends traveling together, or even a cat looking out from its carrier (meow!). Each stop brings new passengers, and each departure feels like a mini-celebration, as the train driver starts the journey again.

At each station, the driver has to bring the train to a complete stop, opening the doors so passengers can get on or off safely. They always check that everyone is on board and seated before closing the doors and heading to the next stop. Just like a roller coaster has a start and finish, the train driver knows every stop on the line, making sure they don't miss a single one.

Feeling the Power of the Engine

Have you ever been near a train and felt it roar by with that deep rumbling sound? That's the power of the train's engine at work! For a train driver, feeling the engine come to life is one of the coolest parts of the job. Trains are powered in different ways —some run on electricity, some use diesel fuel, and some older ones even run on steam! The driver understands every part of the engine, from the mighty wheels to the powerful motor that makes everything move.

When the driver presses the throttle, the engine sends energy to the wheels, which grip the tracks and make the train roll forward. It's a feeling like no other, knowing that you're guiding such a huge, powerful machine. Train drivers say it's like having a superpower!

Staying Calm Under Pressure

Being a train driver also means staying cool and calm, even when things get tricky. Sometimes there might be a delay, or maybe a storm passes through, and the rain makes the tracks slippery.

In those moments, a train driver has to be extra careful, using the brakes and throttle gently to keep everyone safe. If something unexpected happens, like a branch on the tracks, the driver quickly contacts the dispatcher and follows instructions to make sure no one is in danger.

The driver's ability to stay calm keeps passengers relaxed too. They might not know it, but the driver is always making quick decisions to keep the journey smooth and safe. This focus is what makes them great at their job!

Driving a train isn't just about controlling a machine; it's about guiding a journey. It's about taking people places, being responsible, and having fun all at once. Kids who dream of being train drivers know it's a big responsibility, but with each chug of the engine and each toot of the horn, they know they'd be making people's lives better—one station at a time.

So, as you finish this chapter, imagine yourself at the front of a train, pulling the throttle, feeling the engine come alive, and guiding your passengers on their journey. Someday, it could be you making announcements, pressing those buttons, and seeing the world from the best seat on the tracks.

During the rest of this book we will learn more about all aspects of trains, train driving, tracks and much much more. Enjoy!

2: The Different Types Of Trains

Trains aren't just big machines that move along tracks—they come in all shapes, sizes, and types, each with a special job and story. From sleek high-speed trains zooming across countries to the mighty steam engines of the past, each type of train has something incredible to offer.

Passenger Trains: The People Movers

Passenger trains are like giant buses on rails, specially designed to carry people from one place to another. Imagine you're hopping on a passenger train to visit your grandma in the next town, or even traveling across the country on a fun, overnight train trip! Passenger trains are made for comfort, with cozy seats, sometimes even beds, and plenty of windows so you can watch the world whiz by as you travel.

There are several types of passenger trains, including:

Commuter Trains: These trains are perfect for short trips within cities or nearby towns. They make multiple stops to pick up and drop off passengers quickly, just like a bus would. These are popular with people going to work or school each day. Intercity Trains: When you want to go a little further—maybe from one big city to another—you'd take an intercity train. They're designed for longer trips, so they often have more comfortable seats, and some even have snack bars! Overnight Trains: For long-distance trips, sometimes even across countries, you might find yourself on an overnight train. These are exciting because they have sleeper cars with bunk beds where you can rest while the train rocks you to sleep. Imagine waking up in a whole new place!

Passenger trains are all about comfort, speed, and keeping people safe as they travel. These trains are like homes on wheels, carrying hundreds of people to their destinations every day.

Freight Trains: The Strong and Mighty Haulers

While passenger trains are busy transporting people, freight trains have a very different job—they carry things! Freight trains are the heavy lifters of the railway world, built to haul massive loads of cargo over long distances.

Here's what makes freight trains unique:

Power and Strength: Freight trains are long and made up of many cars, each loaded with goods. One train can carry thousands of tons of cargo!

This means they need extra-strong engines to pull all that weight. Different Kinds of Cargo: Freight trains can carry almost anything —grain, coal, cars, furniture, toys, even parts of airplanes! Special cars are used for different cargo. For example, refrigerated cars keep food fresh, while flat cars carry big items like machinery or cars. Less Speed, More Power: Freight trains don't move as fast as passenger trains, but that's okay—they're all about power, not speed. Their job is to keep chugging along steadily, carrying goods from factories to stores, farms to markets, and more.

Freight trains are the backbone of industry, working hard behind the scenes to keep our shelves stocked, our homes warm, and our food fresh. The next time you see a freight train, try counting all the different cars and imagining what treasures they might be carrying inside!

High-Speed Trains: The Speed Demons of the Rails

Now, hold on tight, because here come the high-speed trains! These trains are designed for one thing: speed. High-speed trains zoom along tracks at speeds of over 200 miles per hour—faster than most cars on the highway.

High-speed trains are built very differently from other trains. Here's what makes them special: Aerodynamic Shape: High-speed trains are sleek and have a shape like a bullet or a jet to help them slice through the air with little resistance. This shape helps them go faster with less energy. Dedicated Tracks: Not just any track can handle a high-speed train. These trains have their own special, super-smooth tracks that allow them to glide without bumps or obstacles. These tracks are also carefully guarded to keep animals, people, and other objects away. Advanced Technology: High-speed trains use cutting-edge technology, including powerful electric engines, automatic brakes, and even computers that help drivers make the journey as fast and smooth as possible. Some high-speed trains, like Japan's famous Shinkansen (bullet train), even have the ability to tilt slightly on curves, keeping them steady at high speeds.

Imagine riding on a high-speed train and watching the landscape flash by like a fast-moving movie. You'd reach far-off destinations in just a few hours, making high-speed trains a popular choice for long-distance travellers. In fact, these trains are so quick that they sometimes beat airplanes for certain trips!

Historic Steam Engines: The Giants of the Past

Let's go back in time to when trains were powered by steam! Steam engines are some of the most magical and legendary trains in history, known for their puffs of steam, loud whistles, and big, chugging sounds. These trains ran on steam power, which means they needed water, fire, and coal to get moving.

Here's how steam engines worked: Boiling Water Power: A steam engine is like a big teapot! Inside, water was heated in a giant boiler until it turned into steam. This steam was then released into pistons, which pushed the wheels and made the train move. Coal and Fire: To make the water boil, steam engines needed a lot of heat, which came from burning coal. A special person called a fireman shovelled coal into the firebox, keeping the fire hot so the engine could chug along. The Smoke and Steam Show: As the train moved, it would puff out clouds of steam and smoke from its smokestack. This made steam engines look as if they were breathing, like living giants on wheels!

Though steam engines aren't used as much today, they are still celebrated as symbols of adventure and exploration. These "iron horses" played a huge role in shaping our modern world, helping people travel and trade across long distances. Many museums and tourist spots still have working steam trains, giving people a chance to experience the thrill of riding these mighty machines.

With all these types of trains, you might even be inspired to imagine your own train design. Would it be a passenger train, a freight hauler, or a high-speed bullet train? Whatever you dream up, remember that trains are all about the journey—and every type of train has its own special journey to make.

So, young train driver, now that you know the different types of trains, let's keep learning! Because next time, we'll get to step inside the train cab and see all the cool controls that a train driver gets to use every day. The adventure on the tracks has just begun!

3: Inside The Train Cab

Welcome to the driver's cab, the heart and brain of the train! This is where all the action happens, where the driver works their magic to make the train go, stop, and glide along the tracks. Think of the cab as the train driver's very own office, filled with all kinds of gadgets, levers, and buttons that help control every part of the journey. If you've ever wondered what it's like to sit in the driver's seat of a train, get ready!

The Driver's Seat: Front Row on the Rails

The first thing you'll notice when you climb into the train cab is the driver's seat. This isn't just any old chair—it's a comfy, sturdy seat right up front, giving the driver the best view of the tracks stretching far into the distance. From here, the driver can see signals, other trains, tunnels, and bridges, always keeping an eye on what's up ahead. Some seats are even adjustable, so the driver can move it up, down, forward, or backward to get the perfect view.

In front of the seat lies the control panel, the real heart of the cab. Packed with lights, levers, buttons, and screens, this panel is like a giant remote control for the whole train. Each part has its own special job, and every button is there for a reason. Let's take a look at the main controls that the driver uses to keep everything running smoothly.

Meet the Big Three: Throttle, Brake, and Reverser

In the driver's cab, there are three main controls that every driver uses to start, stop, and steer the train. These are the Throttle, Brake, and Reverser.

The Throttle: This is like the train's "go" button. The throttle is what makes the train speed up. When the driver wants to get moving, they push the throttle forward, and the train starts rolling. The further forward the driver pushes it, the faster the train will go. But it's not just about going fast—the driver has to use the throttle carefully to keep the train moving at a safe, steady speed.

The Brake: Just like in a car, the brake is what slows the train down. But trains are much heavier than cars, so stopping them takes a lot more planning. Instead of a pedal, train drivers use a big lever for the brake, pulling it back to slow down or come to a full stop. The brake is super important, especially when coming into busy stations or approaching red signals.

The Reverser: Have you ever driven a toy train backward on the tracks? The reverser lets real trains do the same thing! It's a lever that tells the train which direction to go: forward, backward, or neutral (meaning the train is stopped). The reverser is key when drivers need to switch tracks or move the train back just a little bit.

Together, these three controls—the throttle, brake, and reverser—are what make the train go, stop, and switch directions. Drivers practice using them all together so the train can move smoothly without any sudden jerks or stops.

Buttons and Levers: The Driver's Tools of the Trade

Aside from the big three controls, there are plenty of other buttons, dials, and levers in the cab that help the driver keep the train running safely. Let's check out some of the coolest ones!

Horn Button: The horn is one of the most recognizable parts of a train. With the press of a button, the driver can sound the train's horn to let people and other trains know they're coming. It's like saying, "Watch out! The train is on the move!" Horns are especially useful at crossings, tunnels, and stations, where the driver needs to make sure everyone hears them coming.

Speedometer: Just like in a car, the train has a speedometer that shows how fast it's going. Drivers must keep an eye on this at all times, making sure the train doesn't go faster than the speed limit. High-speed trains can go incredibly fast, but there are speed limits in cities, towns, and near sharp turns to keep passengers safe.

Signal Lights and Indicators: In the cab, drivers have special lights and indicators that show the status of the train and track ahead. For example, a green light means "Go," while a red light means "Stop." There are also indicators for things like open doors, emergency brakes, and track conditions. These lights help the driver stay informed without having to leave the cab.

Deadman's Pedal: This one has a funny name, but it's actually a very serious safety feature. The deadman's pedal (or sometimes a handle) must be pressed at all times while the train is moving. If the driver lets go, the train will automatically stop. This feature is there in case the driver needs to step away, making sure the train doesn't move without them.

Radio and Communication System: Train drivers don't work alone —they have to stay in contact with the train dispatcher and other crew members. The radio lets drivers communicate important messages, like if they're delayed or if there's something blocking the track. It's a bit like a walkie-talkie, and it's crucial for keeping the journey safe.

Digital Screens: The Train's Dashboard

In newer trains, drivers also have digital screens that show them everything happening with the train. These screens are like a high-tech dashboard, showing things like fuel levels, power usage, and even a map of the tracks. Some screens also show weather conditions and track signals up ahead, helping the driver plan for what's coming next. These screens make it easier to manage the train, giving drivers important information at a glance.

Safety First: Automatic Brakes and Emergency Stops

Trains are designed with lots of safety features to make sure that passengers are safe, no matter what. One of the most important features is the automatic brake system. If the train is going too fast or if it's getting close to another train, the automatic brakes kick in to slow it down. There's also an emergency brake that drivers can pull to stop the train immediately in case of danger.

Using these brakes isn't something drivers do lightly; they only pull the emergency brake in a real emergency. When the brake is pulled, it signals to the train and the crew that there's a problem, helping everyone stay safe.

The Train's Brain: Computerized Controls

In modern trains, much of the cab's technology is connected to computers that help drivers keep everything under control. These computers track the train's speed, distance to the next station, and even how much power it's using. They're like co-pilots for the driver, offering helpful information and even suggesting when to speed up or slow down. This makes it easier for drivers to focus on what's ahead, trusting the computer to keep track of the smaller details.

For every kid who dreams of driving a train, the cab is where that dream becomes a reality. It's where they learn to respect the power of the train, to guide it smoothly on its journey, and to keep everyone on board safe and happy. When you step into the cab, you're stepping into the shoes of a driver—one of the coolest, most important jobs on the rails.

Now that you've peeked into the cab and learned about the amazing controls, get ready, because in the next chapter, we're hitting the tracks! We'll explore the railway network, where tracks crisscross the country like a giant spiderweb, guiding trains on their way to exciting places. The adventure has just begun!

4: The Train Track Network

Welcome to the vast and amazing world of train tracks! If you've ever looked out the window of a train or watched a train from a platform, you know that tracks seem to go on forever, crossing over each other, branching off, or running side-by-side. But how do trains know where to go? And how do they avoid bumping into each other? The answer is in the carefully designed train track network, a giant puzzle of tracks, switches, and signals that keeps everything moving smoothly. Let's jump right in and explore the maze that keeps trains on the right path!

The Basics: Rails, Ties, and Ballast

Before we get into the complicated stuff, let's start with the basics of what makes up a train track. The main parts of a track include:

Rails: These are the long, metal bars that the train wheels ride on. They're made of steel, which is incredibly strong and can handle the weight of a fully loaded train. Rails are laid out in parallel pairs to keep trains stable and moving in a straight line.

Ties (Sleepers): Rails need support to stay in place, and that's where ties come in. Ties are the thick wooden or concrete beams that run underneath and across the rails, holding them steady. They're usually spaced evenly, giving the track that classic railroad look.

Ballast: Underneath the ties, you'll find a layer of crushed stones called ballast. The ballast helps keep everything in place, absorbing vibrations from the train and allowing water to drain away so the track doesn't get flooded or damaged.

Together, these pieces make a strong, sturdy path that trains can follow, from the smallest commuter train to the heaviest freight hauler.

Following the Path: How Trains Stay on Track

One amazing thing about trains is that they're built to stay on their tracks no matter how fast they go or how sharp the curve is. This happens because of flanged wheels—train wheels have a small lip, or flange, on the inside edge that locks onto the rails, preventing the train from sliding off. The wheels guide the train forward and keep it steady on the track.

Unlike cars that have steering wheels to turn, trains can only go where the track takes them. This is why the track network is so important: it tells each train exactly where to go and prevents them from getting lost or ending up on the wrong line.

The Maze of Tracks: Different Paths for Different Trains

In busy areas, like cities or large train stations, tracks can look like a giant spiderweb, crisscrossing in every direction. This can get confusing, but every part of the maze has a purpose! Here's how it all works:

Main Lines: These are the primary tracks that connect big cities and important locations. They're like highways for trains, carrying them over long distances at higher speeds.

Branch Lines: Branch lines are smaller tracks that break off from the main lines. These tracks connect smaller towns, rural areas, or specific factories and warehouses.

Sidings: Sidings are short tracks located alongside main lines. Trains use sidings to pull over and wait if they need to let another train pass. Imagine a passing lane on the highway—that's kind of how sidings work!

Each of these tracks plays a role in the train's journey, guiding it along a path that's safe, fast, and organized. With so many trains on the tracks, it's a good thing there's a plan!

Switches or points: The Train's GPS

Sometimes, a train needs to switch from one track to another to get where it's going. This is where switches, also known as points, come in. A switch or a point is a clever device that lets a train change tracks without stopping. It's a bit like the train's version of a GPS, steering it in the right direction.

Here's how switches / points work: When a train approaches a switch, the driver slows down just a little bit. Inside the switch, a moving piece of rail called a point shifts into place, guiding the train wheels onto a new path. If the point is lined up with the left track, the train will follow that path; if it's lined up with the right track, the train will go that way instead.

Switches can be controlled manually by a track worker or remotely by the train dispatcher, who watches the network from a control centre. For big, busy stations, there might be dozens of switches helping trains find their way in and out of platforms safely.

Signals: The Traffic Lights of the Tracks

In a world where trains follow fixed paths and don't have steering wheels, you might wonder how they avoid running into each other. The answer is signals, the colourful lights along the track that guide trains, just like traffic lights guide cars.

There are three main types of signals: Green: This signal means "go." The track ahead is clear, and the train can keep moving at its current speed. Yellow: A yellow signal means "caution." It warns the driver to slow down because there's something up ahead that might require them to stop, like another train or a switch. Red: A red signal means "stop." The track ahead is blocked, and the train must wait until the signal changes.

Signals are carefully timed and placed to keep trains spaced apart, making sure there's always a safe distance between them. Each signal is controlled by the train dispatcher, who can monitor and adjust them from the control centre if needed.

Stations: Where Tracks Meet and Passengers Board

Stations are some of the most exciting and busiest places along the track network. They're like train hubs, where people get on and off, and trains connect with other lines. Each station is unique, with different kinds of tracks and platforms to handle all the comings and goings.

Here's what you might find at a station:

Platforms: These are the areas where passengers wait to board the train. Platforms are usually level with the train doors, making it easy to step on and off.

Tracks and Sidings: Larger stations have multiple tracks and sidings to handle lots of trains at once. This way, passenger trains, freight trains, and high-speed trains can all arrive and leave without delays.

Signal Boxes: Some stations have signal boxes, little rooms where workers control the local switches and signals, keeping everything organized and on time.

Stations are places of excitement and movement, full of people, luggage, and the sound of train whistles. Each one is part of the network, helping connect passengers to their destinations.

The Dispatcher: The Brain Behind the Tracks

In a busy train system, someone has to make sure everything runs smoothly. That's the job of the train dispatcher. The dispatcher is like a super coach, directing all the trains on the network, setting up signals, and making sure every train stays on schedule. Dispatchers work from a central control centre filled with big screens that show the location of every train on the network.

Dispatchers make quick decisions, like when to let a faster train pass a slower one or when to hold a train to avoid a delay. They communicate with drivers by radio, giving them instructions and making sure everyone's safe. If there's bad weather or an obstacle on the track, dispatchers help figure out a new plan, keeping the network running smoothly even when things get tricky.

5: How Does A Train Move?

Trains are big, powerful machines that can carry hundreds of people, but what gives them the power to move?

The Basics: Energy in Motion

To get a car, a bike, or even a toy car to go, you need energy. Energy is like the fuel for movement. On a bike, the energy comes from your muscles as you pedal; in a car, it comes from petrol. For trains, energy can come from several sources: electricity, diesel fuel, or steam. Each one works a bit differently, but they all do the same thing—they turn energy into motion, helping trains travel down the tracks.

1. Electric Trains: Power from the Wires

Electric trains are the quiet and super-efficient stars of the modern railway. These trains don't have big, noisy engines; instead, they use electricity to power their motors. You might have seen electric trains on commuter lines or even high-speed rail systems. These trains are often connected to overhead wires or a third rail along the track, which supplies them with the electricity they need to zoom along.

Here's how electric trains work: Power from the Wires: The train gets its energy from an electric current flowing through overhead wires or a rail on the ground. This current flows into the train through a device called a pantograph (which touches the overhead wire) or a third-rail shoe (which connects to the third rail). Electric Motors: Inside the train, the electric current powers electric motors. These motors are like powerful magnets that spin the train's wheels, converting electricity into movement. Speed Control: The driver can control the speed by adjusting how much electricity flows to the motors. More electricity makes the wheels spin faster, while less electricity slows the train down.

Electric trains are popular because they're quiet, clean, and very efficient. Since they don't burn any fuel, they don't release smoke or pollution, which is better for the environment. And because they're so quiet, they're great for use in cities where noise levels need to be low. Riding an electric train feels almost like gliding along the tracks, with no rumbling or roaring, just a smooth and speedy journey!

2. Diesel Trains: Power from Fuel

Next up, we have diesel trains. These trains don't rely on electricity from the outside; instead, they carry their power source with them in the form of diesel fuel. If you've ever seen a big, rumbling train with smoke coming out of the top, it was probably a diesel train. Diesel trains are strong and can travel long distances without needing wires or special tracks, making them ideal for journeys across remote areas where electric lines might not reach.

Here's how diesel trains work: Diesel Engine: A diesel train has a powerful diesel engine, much like a car engine but much bigger and stronger. The engine burns diesel fuel to produce energy, which creates motion. Electric Generator: When the diesel engine burns fuel, it turns a big generator that creates electricity. So, in a way, diesel trains also use electricity, but they make their own instead of drawing it from wires. Electric Motors: Just like in an electric train, this electricity is sent to the electric motors, which then turn the train's wheels.

Diesel trains are great because they can go anywhere there are tracks, even places where it's too expensive or difficult to build electric lines. They're especially useful for freight trains that carry heavy loads across long distances. However, unlike electric trains, diesel trains release smoke and pollution from the fuel they burn, which is why more and more railways are switching to electric power. Still, diesel trains are some of the hardest-working machines on the rails, carrying everything from people to entire loads of cars, coal, and other big cargo!

3. Steam Trains: Power from Water and Fire

Now, let's travel back in time to the age of the steam train. Steam trains were the first type of train ever invented, and they used a very different kind of power—steam. Steam trains are what you might think of when you imagine a classic train with big, puffy clouds of smoke and a loud "choo-choo" sound. These trains don't use electricity or diesel fuel; instead, they rely on the power of boiling water!

Here's how steam trains work: Fire and Coal: To create steam, the train needs a fire. In the old days, workers called firemen would shovel coal into a firebox to keep the fire burning hot.
Boiler and Water: Above the fire is a large tank, or boiler, filled with water. The fire heats the water, turning it into steam. Steam is created when water boils and turns into gas, building up a lot of pressure. Steam Pistons: This steam is then funnelled into pistons, which are like giant pushers that make the train's wheels move. The pressure from the steam pushes the pistons back and forth, and this motion turns the wheels, making the train go forward. Chugging and Puffing: Every time the steam pushes out, it escapes through the smokestack, making that classic chugging sound and releasing puffs of steam and smoke.

Steam trains were revolutionary when they were invented. They could go much faster than horse-drawn wagons and could carry more cargo over longer distances. Although they're no longer used for regular travel, steam trains are still celebrated for their charm, history, and the impressive engineering that makes them work. Some places still run steam trains for fun, so people can experience the joy of riding a train that breathes and chugs like a living thing!

Moving Forward: Trains of the Future

As technology keeps advancing, scientists and engineers are coming up with new ways to make trains move faster, quieter, and more environmentally friendly. Some of the trains of the future include:

Maglev Trains: These high-tech trains don't use wheels at all! Instead, they float just above the track, thanks to powerful magnets. This reduces friction, allowing them to reach speeds over 300 miles per hour. Maglev trains are super smooth and ultra-fast, making them the future of high-speed rail.

Hydrogen Trains: Imagine a train that runs on nothing but water! Hydrogen trains use a fuel cell that combines hydrogen and oxygen to create electricity, with only water as a byproduct. This means no pollution, just clean energy powering the train.

Solar-Powered Trains: Some trains are being designed to use solar panels, collecting energy from the sun. This type of train can run on sunny days without needing fuel or electricity from outside sources.

Next Time You're on a Train...

Now that you know how trains move, the next time you're riding a train, try to imagine what's happening underneath you. Think about the motors humming in an electric train, the roar of the diesel engine, or the chugging power of a steam engine. Remember, each train has its own special way of moving, guided by science, engineering, and lots of energy.

6: Train Signals And Safety Lights

Trains are big, fast, and incredibly powerful machines, so keeping them safe on the tracks is essential. The railway network is like a giant, carefully choreographed dance, with each train knowing exactly when and where to go. But with so many trains on the tracks, how do they avoid bumping into each other? The answer is train signals and safety lights! These signals act like traffic lights for trains, guiding them on when to go, slow down, or stop.

The Colours of Safety: Red, Yellow, and Green Signals

Train signals are color-coded lights that tell drivers what to do as they travel along the tracks. Just like traffic lights, they use three main colours:

1. Green: Go! When the signal light is green, it tells the driver that the track ahead is clear, and they can move forward. A green signal means it's safe to keep up their current speed.

2. Yellow: Caution! A yellow signal warns the driver to slow down and be ready to stop. There might be another train ahead, a switch,

or a red signal up ahead. It's like saying, "Be careful and stay alert!"

3. Red: Stop! A red signal means the train must come to a full stop and wait. The track ahead might be blocked, or it could be a busy area like a station. Red lights are crucial for keeping trains spaced apart and safe.

Train signals are placed along the track at regular intervals, and each one helps guide the driver safely along the path, avoiding potential accidents.

Types of Signals: Different Ways to Communicate

There are different kinds of signals, each with its own job. Here are some common ones:

Block Signals: The track is divided into sections, called blocks. Block signals tell the driver if the block ahead is clear or occupied by another train. This helps keep trains spaced apart, making sure they don't get too close to each other.

Junction Signals: These signals guide trains through junctions, where tracks split or come together. Junction signals tell the driver which direction to go and if the junction is clear.

Platform Signals: These are found at stations and help guide trains in and out of platforms safely. They also let drivers know when it's safe to close the doors and depart.

Speed Restriction Signals: Sometimes, trains need to slow down for safety, like when they're going around a sharp curve or passing through a work zone. Speed restriction signals tell the driver the maximum safe speed for that section of the track.

How Signals Work: The Dispatcher's Role

Signals don't work on their own; they're controlled by a person called the dispatcher. The dispatcher watches over the entire railway network from a control centre, monitoring the locations and movements of each train. They use computers and maps to keep everything organized, adjusting signals when needed.

For example, if one train is delayed, the dispatcher might adjust nearby signals to keep other trains from getting too close. The dispatcher and the signals work together, guiding each train safely along its journey.

Automatic Signals: Helping Trains Stay Safe

In modern rail systems, many signals are automatic, meaning they change without a dispatcher's help. Automatic signals use sensors on the tracks to detect if a train is in a specific section. When the train leaves, the sensor "tells" the signal to turn green, allowing the next train to pass. This makes the railway network more efficient and keeps trains moving smoothly.

Special Lights and Safety Measures

Alongside signals, there are other safety features that help keep trains and their passengers safe:

Crossing Signals: When a train is approaching a level crossing (where a road crosses the tracks), crossing signals light up and bells sound to warn cars and pedestrians. Sometimes, gates even lower to block the road, making sure no one is in the way as the train passes.

Deadman's Switch: As mentioned earlier in the book, this safety feature ensures that the driver is always alert. The driver has to keep a button or pedal pressed down while the train is moving. If they let go, the train will automatically stop, preventing accidents in case of an emergency.

Cab Signaling: In some high-speed trains, the signals are displayed inside the driver's cab rather than along the track. This makes it easier for drivers to see the signals at high speeds, without missing anything important.

Why Signals Matter: The Big Picture of Safety

Train signals and safety lights are essential because they allow trains to share the tracks safely, even when they're traveling at high speeds or in busy areas. Imagine a world where each train was on its own, with no signals to guide it—it would be like cars driving on highways without any traffic lights or signs! Signals make sure that every train knows when to go, when to slow down, and when to stop.

Next time you're near a railway crossing or riding a train, look out for these signals and lights. Remember, they're not just there to flash pretty colors; they're there to keep everyone safe, working together like a team of invisible traffic controllers.

So, now you know what makes trains move and how signals keep them on track. These two pieces—the power of the engine and the guidance of the signals—are what make trains one of the safest and most efficient ways to travel. Every time a train glides down the tracks, it's not just a single machine in motion; it's a carefully choreographed dance of energy, control, and safety. The engine provides the power, and the signals provide the direction, making sure everyone arrives at their destination safe and sound.

7: Sounds Of The Train: Whistles, Bells, And Horns

Trains are known for their unique and powerful sounds that rumble through stations, echo in the countryside, and call out to everyone nearby. These sounds aren't just noise—they're important signals used by train drivers and engineers to keep passengers, crew, and other trains safe. From the iconic "choo-choo" of a steam train's whistle to the deep, rumbling honk of a modern train horn, each sound tells a story and serves a purpose. Let's explore the orchestra of sounds that make trains so unique, learning what each one means and how they keep the railway humming smoothly.

The Classic Train Whistle: The Voice of the Steam Train

The first sound people think of when they hear "train" is often the whistle of an old steam engine. That "choo-choo" or "woo-woo" sound is part of railway history and brings to mind images of vintage steam trains puffing through the countryside. But what exactly is a train whistle, and why do steam trains have them?

How the Whistle Works

A steam train whistle works like a giant metal whistle. Here's how it happens:

Steam Power: When the driver pulls a lever in the cab, steam from the boiler is released into the whistle. Sound Waves: The steam rushes through the whistle's bell (the hollow tube), creating sound waves. The whistle's shape and size determine the pitch of the sound, whether it's high or low.

The steam whistle is both musical and functional. It's loud enough to be heard from miles away, alerting everyone nearby that a train is coming. Each steam train's whistle can have its own distinct tone, meaning different engines make different sounds!

What the Whistle Signals

Steam whistles were used as signals long before electric horns and bells. Here are a few common uses: Two Short Blasts: The train is ready to start moving forward. One Long Blast: A warning to people or animals on or near the tracks. Three Short Blasts: The train is about to back up. A Series of Short Blasts: This is the "danger" signal, meaning there's an emergency or obstruction on the tracks.

Steam whistles aren't as common today, but on historic trains and scenic routes, you might still hear their melodic call. It's a reminder of a time when trains were the fastest way to travel and every whistle meant something special.

The Mighty Horn: The Modern Train's Call

Today, most trains use horns rather than whistles. Train horns are larger, louder, and designed for the diesel and electric engines used in modern railways. You've probably heard a train horn's deep, booming sound, especially if you live near a railroad crossing or train station. Unlike the steam whistle's classic "choo-choo," train horns produce a powerful honk that gets people's attention immediately.

How the Horn Works
Train horns work differently from steam whistles because they don't rely on steam. Here's how they function: Compressed Air: Modern train horns use compressed air. When the driver pushes a button or pulls a lever, this compressed air is forced through a diaphragm inside the horn. Vibration: The air makes the diaphragm vibrate, creating sound waves that travel through the horn and produce a loud honking sound. Different Tones: Some trains have multiple horns that play together, creating a chord (a mix of different notes). This makes the sound fuller and more attention-grabbing.

Train horns are designed to be loud and impossible to ignore. They play a huge role in railway safety, especially at crossings, where they remind everyone to stay clear of the tracks.

Bells:

Alongside whistles and horns, many trains also have bells. Train bells don't have the same booming volume as horns, but they have an important role in safety, especially in stations and crowded areas. The sound of a train bell is more like a friendly jingle, letting people know that the train is about to move or that it's coming into the station.

How the Bell Works
Train bells are usually mechanical or electric, depending on the train type: Mechanical Bells: Older trains and some modern trains use mechanical bells, which are activated by pulling a cord or pressing a button. This makes a hammer strike the bell repeatedly, creating a clear, ringing sound. Electric Bells: Electric bells are controlled with a switch and use electricity to ring the bell automatically.

What the Bell Signals
The bell on a train isn't as loud as a horn, so it's typically used in quieter or more crowded areas. Here are some times when you might hear a train's bell: Departing the Station: The bell rings to let everyone know the train is about to start moving. Approaching a Platform or Crossing: Bells warn people at a station or crossing that the train is near and to stay clear. Moving Through Crowded Areas: In busy or urban areas, drivers often ring the bell to remind pedestrians and cars to stay alert.

While the horn might shout a warning, the bell is more like a gentle reminder, making it a key part of the train's safety system.

Fun Fact: Different Countries, Different Sounds

Trains all over the world use sounds, but the signals can be slightly different depending on where you are: In the United States: Trains often use the specific four-blast pattern at crossings (two long, one short, one long). In the United Kingdom: Train horns are often shorter and less complex, and train bells aren't as commonly used. In Japan: High-speed trains like the Shinkansen have quieter horns to reduce noise pollution, but they're still loud enough for safety!

8: Picking Up And Dropping Off Passengers

One of the most exciting parts of a train driver's job is picking up and dropping off passengers. Whether it's the cheerful chatter of kids heading on a school trip, travellers with big suitcases ready for adventures, or commuters heading home after a long day, train stations are buzzing with energy! But behind the excitement, there's a lot of careful work involved. Today, we'll dive into the art of stopping at stations, opening doors safely, and making sure every passenger boards and exits smoothly.

The Approach: Timing the Perfect Stop

Imagine driving a train that's over 1,000 feet long, weighing as much as 400 cars combined. Now, picture pulling that train to a gentle, precise stop at a busy station platform filled with passengers waiting to board. It's not an easy task! Train drivers rely on a mix of skill, timing, and technology to stop their trains smoothly and accurately.

Planning Ahead

To make a smooth and timely stop, a train driver starts planning the approach well in advance. They monitor their speed, the distance to the platform, and any signals along the track. Since trains take much longer to slow down than cars, drivers begin braking far away from the station, sometimes up to half a mile in advance!

Slowing Down Gradually: As the train nears the station, the driver applies gentle braking to slow down gradually. This helps avoid sudden jerks that could throw passengers off balance. Checking the Speedometer: Train drivers watch their speed closely, making sure it's safe and steady for entering the station. Each station might have different speed limits, depending on how busy it is and how long the platform is.

By the time the train reaches the platform, it's already slowing to a steady pace, ready to make a smooth and comfortable stop.

The Final Stop: Precision Parking. As the train reaches the end of the platform, the driver applies the brakes more firmly, bringing it to a complete halt. But stopping isn't as simple as it sounds; the driver has to make sure the train lines up perfectly with the platform so that every door is accessible for passengers.

Platform Markings: Most stations have markings on the platform to help drivers align their trains. These might include signs, painted lines, or numbered markers showing exactly where to stop. Some platforms even have electronic indicators or mirrors to help drivers see the entire length of the train.
Perfect Positioning: Positioning is key—if the train is too far forward or backward, some doors may not align with the platform, making it harder for passengers to board and exit.

After the perfect stop, it's time to open the doors and welcome everyone aboard!

Opening the Doors: Ensuring Passenger Safety

Once the train is stopped and secure, it's time to open the doors. This sounds simple, but it's actually a well-coordinated process designed to keep everyone safe and comfortable.

In the driver's cab, there's a control panel specifically for the doors. With just a press of a button, the driver can open or close all the doors on either side of the train. But there's a catch: the doors only open on the side facing the platform, never on the opposite side, which might be dangerous if it opens onto a busy track.

Side Selection: Before opening the doors, the driver selects which side to open. If the platform is on the left, the doors on the left side open, while the doors on the right stay locked. The same process works for a platform on the right. Safety Sensors: Many modern trains have sensors on their doors to detect if something (or someone) is stuck. If the sensors detect an object, like a bag or a hand, the doors won't close until it's clear, keeping everyone safe.

The All-Clear Signal. After opening the doors, the driver waits for a signal from the conductor or platform staff indicating that it's safe for passengers to board and exit. This signal might be a wave, a thumbs-up, or even a green light on the control panel. In some cases, there might be an announcement over the station speakers, letting everyone know that boarding is ready to begin.

With the doors open, passengers can now step onto the train. But there's still plenty of work to ensure that everyone boards safely and comfortably. Here's how it all works: Modern trains are designed to make boarding easy for everyone, including people with disabilities, families with strollers, and travelers with heavy luggage. Many stations have step-free platforms that align perfectly with the train, so passengers don't have to climb any steps.

Ramps and Lifts: Some trains are equipped with ramps or lifts for passengers who need extra assistance. Train staff or station employees can help deploy these ramps, making it easier for people in wheelchairs or with limited mobility to board smoothly. Automatic Door Warnings: To prevent people from accidentally stepping into a closing door, some trains have automatic lights or beeps that alert passengers when doors are about to close.

Allowing Time for All Passengers. Each station stop is timed, but train drivers and conductors always make sure to give passengers enough time to board safely. They keep an eye on the platform to ensure everyone, including the last-minute runners, has a chance to get on.

On the Platform: Safety Reminders and Signals. For passengers waiting to board, the platform is an exciting but busy place. Here are a few safety measures and signals that help keep things organized:

Yellow Lines: Platforms often have a yellow line along the edge, marking a safe distance from the tracks. Passengers are encouraged to stay behind this line until the train is fully stopped. Station Announcements: Speakers at the station announce when trains are arriving, departing, or delayed. They also provide reminders for passengers to stand clear of the doors and hold onto their belongings. Mind the Gap: You'll often hear the phrase "Mind the Gap" as a reminder to watch the small space between the train and the platform. Even with step-free platforms, there can be a small gap, so passengers are advised to step carefully when boarding or exiting.

Dropping Off Passengers: Smooth Departures. Once everyone has boarded, it's time to close the doors and get back on the tracks. But before the train pulls out of the station, the driver checks to make sure all passengers have safely exited as well. Here's what happens:

Checking the Platform. The driver and conductor check the platform to make sure no one is rushing toward the train at the last second. They also look to see that all passengers have exited safely and that no one is lingering too close to the doors or tracks.

Closing the Doors. When the platform is clear, the driver presses the button to close the doors. Some trains have a chime or beep that sounds just before the doors close, giving passengers a final heads-up.

Door Interlock: On many trains, a safety system called the door interlock prevents the train from moving if any door is open. This ensures that the train won't accidentally start moving while someone is still boarding or exiting. Final Checks: The driver double-checks the control panel to make sure all doors are securely closed and locked. Only then are they ready to start the journey to the next station.

Getting Back on Track: Leaving the Station Smoothly. Now that everyone is safely on board or has exited, it's time for the train to pull away from the platform. But just like arriving at the station, leaving requires skill and precision. The driver gently releases the brakes and gradually increases the throttle to avoid jerking the train forward. This smooth departure helps keep passengers comfortable and allows everyone to settle into their seats.

Building Speed Gradually: The driver accelerates gradually, bringing the train up to speed smoothly. This is especially important in busy areas where the next station might be close by. Watching the Signals: Before leaving the station, the driver checks the signals to make sure the track ahead is clear. A green signal means it's safe to proceed, while a yellow or red signal might indicate a need to wait or slow down.

From the careful approach to the well-timed departure, every part of picking up and dropping off passengers is an art form that keeps the railway running smoothly.

9: Nighttime And Daytime Driving

A train driver's job doesn't stop when the sun goes down; trains travel through all hours, whether it's bright and sunny or dark and quiet. Each time of day brings its own challenges and adventures, from the early morning hustle and bustle to the calm, star-lit silence of nighttime. Let's dive into what it's like to drive a train at different times of day and explore the unique tools and techniques that help train drivers stay on track around the clock.

Daytime Driving: Bright, Bustling, and Full of Action

During the day, train stations and tracks are full of activity. Commuters rush to work, families travel for holidays, and students head to school. The tracks are busy with trains of all kinds: passenger trains, freight trains, and high-speed bullet trains zipping from one station to the next. Here's what makes daytime driving unique:

Clear Visibility

During the day, the sun provides natural light that allows drivers to see everything clearly—from the tracks stretching far ahead to signals, signs, and any obstacles that might be near the tracks. Drivers can spot distant signals, read track signs, and see switches from further away, giving them plenty of time to adjust speed or direction.

Seeing Signals and Signs: In daylight, signals are easy to spot and interpret. Green, yellow, and red lights are clear, allowing drivers to respond quickly.

Watching for Obstacles: During the day, the driver has an easier time spotting things like fallen branches, animals, or people near the tracks. Although train tracks are usually fenced off, animals sometimes wander too close, and daylight helps the driver spot them in time.

Dealing with Busy Stations

Daytime is also the busiest time at train stations, especially in the morning and late afternoon when people are commuting. Drivers must be extra alert at stations to make smooth stops, coordinate with station staff, and ensure safe boarding and exiting for all passengers.

Frequent Stops: Daytime trains often make more stops, especially commuter trains. Each stop requires precise control, with the driver gradually slowing down and positioning the train perfectly at the platform.

Platform Crowds: With so many people at stations, the driver, conductor, and platform staff work together to ensure safe boarding and exiting, making announcements and watching for passengers in need of assistance.

Sunlight Challenges

While the sun is helpful for visibility, it can also create challenges, especially during sunrise and sunset when it's lower in the sky.

Glare: Bright sunlight can create glare, which can make it hard for drivers to see signals and track details. Many drivers use sun visors or tinted sunglasses to reduce the glare and keep visibility clear.
Shadowed Tracks: The sun can also create long shadows, especially near tall buildings or trees along the track. These shadows can sometimes hide obstacles or make signals harder to see.

Nighttime Driving: Calm, Quiet, and Filled with Challenges

Once the sun goes down, the railway transforms. Stations quiet down, the surroundings are blanketed in darkness, and the tracks stretch out like mysterious ribbons under the stars. Nighttime driving brings a sense of calm and solitude, but it also requires a unique set of skills and tools to keep everyone safe.

At night, train drivers rely on artificial light sources instead of sunlight to guide them. This means they must be extra alert and make use of special equipment to navigate the tracks.

Train Headlights: Trains are equipped with powerful headlights, which light up the tracks directly in front of them. Unlike car headlights, which shine ahead and to the sides, train headlights are directed straight down the tracks, helping the driver see signals and obstacles along the railway.

Signal Lights Stand Out: One advantage of nighttime driving is that signal lights are more visible in the dark. Red, yellow, and green lights shine brightly, making it easy for drivers to spot and interpret signals, even from a distance.

Trackside Reflectors: Reflective markers and signs along the track help guide the driver by bouncing the light from the train's headlights back toward the cab. These reflectors are especially helpful on curved tracks or in areas with fewer signals.

Nighttime driving requires additional tools to help drivers stay safe and maintain smooth operations. Here are a few tools and techniques that help train drivers naviate the dark:

Cab Lighting: Inside the cab, soft lights provide just enough illumination for the driver to see the controls without ruining their night vision. Night vision is important because it helps the driver see the track and signals without being blinded by bright interior lights.

Digital Displays: Modern trains have screens in the cab that show important information, like the train's speed, distance to the next station, and upcoming signals. These displays are designed to be easily readable in low light, so drivers can stay informed without needing bright lights. Radio Communication: At night, fewer people are around to help if something goes wrong. That's why radio communication with dispatchers and other train crews is essential. The dispatcher can alert drivers to any issues on the track, like maintenance work or animals that have wandered onto the rails.

Nighttime brings a sense of calm to the railway, which can be both relaxing and challenging for train drivers. With fewer trains on the tracks, there's less traffic to worry about, but this calm can sometimes lead to drowsiness. Staying alert is crucial.

Maintaining Focus: At night, drivers use techniques to stay focused, like adjusting their seat position or taking sips of water. Some drivers use the radio to stay connected with dispatchers and other train crews, which helps keep them engaged.
Watching for Wildlife: Animals are more active at night, and they sometimes wander near the tracks. Drivers must stay alert for signs of wildlife and be prepared to slow down if needed.

Two particularly magical and challenging times for train drivers are dawn and dusk. These are times of transition when the light changes quickly, creating beautiful scenes and unique challenges.

Dawn is a special time on the railway. As the sun rises, the world gradually lights up, and trains begin to fill with early morning passengers.

10: The Train Driver's Daily Routine

From the crack of dawn until the final stop of the night, train drivers follow a precise routine to keep their trains moving safely and on time. Each day is filled with checks, controls, and the thrill of guiding hundreds of passengers on their journeys.

Many train drivers start their days early, even before the sun is up. With railways running from dawn until midnight (and sometimes even around the clock), drivers need to be ready for shifts that start at all hours. To keep everything running smoothly, a train driver begins with some important preparation.

1. Arriving at the Depot

The depot is like the train's home base, where trains are stored, inspected, and repaired. Drivers arrive here, often with a cup of coffee in hand, ready for a day on the tracks. The first stop is usually the driver's briefing room.

Briefing and Route Check: The driver checks in to learn about the day's route, any schedule changes, and important information like weather conditions or track work. They may receive a "driver's log," a document listing details about the train, stations, stops, and any unique instructions.

Safety Gear: Train drivers usually have a uniform and safety gear, including a reflective vest, a hard hat, and sometimes even gloves if they'll be inspecting the train. Safety is the priority, and they make sure they're fully prepared before heading to their train.

2. Pre-Departure Inspection

Before a driver can hit the rails, they need to check the train to ensure everything is in perfect working order. This is like a pilot checking an airplane or a captain checking their ship. The train inspection includes:

Exterior Check: The driver walks along the train, looking for any visible issues like loose parts, worn wheels, or dents. They also check the doors to ensure they open and close properly.

Brake Test: Testing the brakes is essential. The driver engages and releases the brakes to make sure they're working smoothly. If the brakes don't work, the train doesn't move!

Lights and Horn: The driver tests the headlights, interior lights, and the horn. Headlights are crucial for visibility, especially during nighttime driving, and the horn is important for safety at crossings.

Once everything checks out, it's time to board the cab and get ready for departure.

With all systems checked, the driver settles into the cab, where they'll spend the next several hours controlling the train. Here's how they get the journey rolling.

3. Setting Up the Cab

The train cab is like the driver's office, and every tool and control needs to be set up correctly. The driver adjusts the seat and mirrors, checks the speedometer, and reviews the route map. They also prepare their communication devices to stay in touch with the dispatcher and conductor throughout the journey.

Setting the Reverser and Throttle: The driver places the reverser (a lever that determines the direction of the train) in "forward" mode and gently adjusts the throttle, the control that determines speed.

Door Control and Announcements: Many drivers also have access to the PA system, where they can make announcements to passengers, welcoming them aboard and providing information about upcoming stops.

With everything ready, it's time to release the brakes and begin the journey!

The Open Rails: Managing the Route and Stopping at Stations

Once the train leaves the station, the driver's day truly begins. While it might seem like they're just steering down the tracks, there's a lot more happening in the cab. Drivers must stay focused on speed, signals, stops, and communication.

4. Following Signals and Maintaining Speed

On the open rails, drivers need to pay close attention to signals and speed limits.

Speed Monitoring: Different sections of the track have different speed limits, and the driver watches the speedometer closely to ensure they're moving at the right pace. High-speed trains, in particular, have strict speed regulations to keep passengers safe.

Signal Watching: Along the route, the driver encounters signal lights—red, yellow, and green. Green means it's safe to go, yellow means caution and slow down, and red means stop. The driver adjusts speed or stops accordingly, maintaining a safe distance from other trains.

5. Stopping at Stations

One of the most important parts of a train driver's job is stopping at stations, where passengers board and exit. Each stop is a precisely timed event, and here's how it happens:

Braking Smoothly: As the train approaches the station, the driver gradually applies the brakes to make a smooth, gentle stop. They aim to line up the doors perfectly with the platform markings so passengers can easily board and exit.

Opening and Closing Doors: Once stopped, the driver opens the doors (usually only on the side facing the platform). The doors remain open until everyone has boarded or exited. Some stations have staff to help, and the driver waits for an "all clear" signal before closing the doors and moving on.

6. Weather Challenges

Weather can affect train travel, and drivers must adjust their routines in rain, snow, fog, or extreme heat.

Rain and Fog: Rain can make tracks slippery, and fog reduces visibility. Drivers use headlights and slow down to navigate safely in these conditions.

Snow and Ice: In winter, ice can make stopping more challenging. Drivers use extra caution, starting to brake earlier than usual to ensure a smooth stop.

7. Radio Communication with Dispatch

Communication with the dispatcher is constant throughout the day. Dispatchers monitor all trains on the tracks and provide updates to drivers about track conditions, signal changes, and any adjustments to the schedule.

Track Work or Obstructions: If there's maintenance work or an unexpected obstacle (like a fallen branch) on the track, the dispatcher informs the driver, who may need to slow down or stop temporarily. Delay Management: If the train is delayed, the driver communicates with the dispatcher and the conductor to keep passengers informed.

Lunchtime and Breaks: Staying Fresh and Focused

Train drivers work long shifts, often up to eight hours or more, so taking breaks is essential. During long routes, drivers have scheduled breaks at specific stations where another driver takes over temporarily, allowing them to rest, grab a snack, and stay alert for the rest of the journey.

8. Staying Energized

Many drivers bring snacks and water to stay energized during their shifts. Some bring along sandwiches, fruit, or trail mix to munch on during breaks at larger stations. Hydration is important, as long hours in the cab can be tiring.

As the day comes to a close, the driver completes the final part of the journey, eventually bringing the train back to its starting point or ending location.

9. Final Passenger Drop-Off

The last station is the end of the line for both the passengers and the driver. At this point, the driver stops the train for the final time, allowing passengers to exit. Once everyone is off, it's time to perform one last set of tasks.

10. Securing the Train

After the final stop, the driver secures the train, ensuring everything is safe and ready for the next driver or for maintenance. This includes:

Powering Down: The driver turns off the throttle, places the reverser in neutral, and engages the parking brake. Final Inspection: They walk through the train, checking for any forgotten items, ensuring all lights are off, and making sure all doors are closed.

Reporting Back: The End-of-Day Routine

The last step in a train driver's day is to return to the depot for a quick debrief.

11. Daily Report and Debrief

Once back at the depot, the driver heads to the briefing room to report any issues encountered during the day. This report includes:

Mechanical Issues: Any problems with the train, such as noisy brakes, flickering lights, or door malfunctions, are noted so maintenance staff can fix them. Delay Report: If there were delays, the driver explains the reason, which helps dispatch and scheduling teams adjust for future journeys.

12. Preparing for the Next Day

Finally, the driver prepares for the next shift or hands over the train to the incoming crew. If they're working again the following day, they may even check the next day's route in advance.

11: Train Stations And The Station Master

Train stations are the bustling heart of the railway system, filled with passengers, the sound of announcements, and the excitement of travel. But behind the scenes, there's a lot happening to keep things running smoothly—and one key person overseeing it all is the station master. Like the conductor of an orchestra, the station master makes sure every train, passenger, and announcement is perfectly timed and coordinated. In this chapter, we'll take a closer look at the role of the station master, how tickets work, and how drivers and station staff communicate to keep everything on track.

Train stations are alive with activity. From the early morning to late at night, people are coming and going—families off on holiday, commuters heading to work, tourists exploring new places, and sometimes even pets on their way to new homes! Each station has its own unique layout, but they all share some common features:

Platforms: These are the areas where trains stop for passengers to board and exit. Platforms are marked with signs indicating where each train and car will be located, making it easy for passengers to find their seats.

Ticket Counters and Machines: Passengers can buy tickets at counters staffed by station employees or from machines located around the station. Tickets are a passport to the train journey, and they come in many types, from single journeys to monthly passes.

Waiting Areas: Many stations have waiting areas for passengers to sit comfortably while they wait for their train. Some larger stations even have cafes, restaurants, and shops.

Departure and Arrival Boards: Large electronic boards display the schedule of trains arriving and departing. These boards update in real-time to let passengers know if their train is on time, delayed, or ready for boarding.

Announcers: You'll often hear station staff making announcements over the loudspeakers, letting passengers know about upcoming trains, platform changes, or other important information.

Stations are more than just places where trains stop—they're hubs where everything comes together, and they're filled with people working hard behind the scenes to keep things moving smoothly.

The Role of the Station Master: The Heart of the Station

At the centre of it all is the station master, a person whose job is to make sure that every train arrives and departs on time and that every passenger has a safe and smooth experience. The station master's role combines leadership, communication, and problem-solving.

Let's break down some of their key responsibilities:

1. Keeping the Station Running Smoothly

The station master oversees all the activities at the station. This includes coordinating with train drivers, conductors, and station staff to make sure everyone knows what they need to do.

Timetable Management: The station master keeps track of the station's timetable, making sure each train arrives and departs at the correct time. If a train is delayed or an extra train needs to be added, the station master is the one who arranges it.

Platform Assignments: Some larger stations have multiple platforms for different train routes. The station master ensures that each train is assigned to the right platform, and that passengers know where to go.

Safety and Order: The station master keeps an eye on the station to make sure everything is safe and orderly. They monitor crowded areas, help with emergency situations, and ensure the station's rules are followed.

2. Communicating with Train Drivers and Conductors

Communication is a huge part of the station master's job. They constantly communicate with train drivers, conductors, and other railway staff. Here's how they work together:

Dispatching Trains: The station master gives the final "all clear" signal for a train to depart. They check to make sure all passengers are safely aboard, the doors are closed, and the platform is clear. Once everything is ready, they signal the driver to start moving.

Radio and Phone Communication: Station masters use radios and phones to stay in touch with drivers. If there's a change in the schedule, a delay, or an issue with the track, the station master relays this information to the driver so they can adjust the journey as needed.

Coordinating with Conductors: Conductors are responsible for onboard safety and passenger service, and they work closely with the station master to keep things organized. For example, if there are special needs passengers, the station master may alert the conductor to ensure they receive assistance.

3. Managing Ticketing and Boarding

Ticketing is another essential part of the station master's job. Making sure each passenger has the correct ticket and is on the right train is crucial for a smooth journey.

Ticket Checks: Station masters may conduct random ticket checks or assign staff to check tickets before passengers board. They help passengers find the right platform or assist with ticket issues.

Ensuring Fair Boarding: On busy days, like holidays, the station master ensures that everyone has a fair chance to board and that people don't overcrowd the train. They may even hold trains for a few extra seconds to allow all passengers to board safely.

Ticketing: Your Key to the Journey

Tickets are more than just slips of paper—they're each passenger's pass to their own unique journey. Here's a quick guide to how tickets work in the train system:

Types of Tickets

Single Journey Ticket: This ticket allows passengers to travel from one station to another without any return trip. It's often used by people going on day trips or traveling for work.

Round-Trip Ticket: For passengers planning to go somewhere and return the same day, a round-trip ticket covers both journeys in one.

Monthly or Annual Passes: Frequent travellers, like commuters, often buy passes that let them travel unlimited times on specific routes within a certain time period.

Digital Tickets: In many modern stations, tickets are now digital. Passengers can use their phones to show an electronic ticket, which makes it faster to board and easier to keep track of.

With a mix of communication skills, leadership, and a keen eye for detail, the station master keeps everything running like clockwork. So next time you're at a train station, take a moment to appreciate the hardworking station master and their team, who make each journey possible. From the first train in the morning to the last ride of the night, they're there to help you reach your destination safely and comfortably.

12: Cargo Trains And Carrying Freight

When we think about trains, we often imagine passenger trains filled with people on their way to work, school, or vacation. But there's another kind of train on the tracks that plays a huge role in our daily lives: cargo trains! These trains don't carry passengers; instead, they transport goods and materials that we use every day, from food to cars to building supplies. Cargo trains, also called freight trains, are like giant moving warehouses, helping transport everything we need across cities, states, and even countries. In this chapter, we'll explore how cargo trains work, the special cars they use, and why they're so essential for keeping our world connected.

The Mighty Role of Cargo Trains

Cargo trains might not get as much attention as passenger trains, but they're just as important—if not more! Every day, they carry massive loads that would be impossible to transport efficiently by truck, boat, or plane alone. Cargo trains can move thousands of tons of goods over long distances in a single trip, making them an economical, environmentally friendly way to ship items.

Without cargo trains, delivering the things we use daily—like food, electronics, and clothes—would be much slower and more expensive.

Why Cargo Trains Are So Important

1. Efficient Transport: Cargo trains are extremely efficient at moving goods across long distances. A single cargo train can carry as much freight as hundreds of trucks! This saves on fuel, reduces road traffic, and lowers the cost of goods.

2. Environmentally Friendly: Trains produce far less pollution per ton of goods transported compared to trucks or planes. This makes cargo trains a greener choice for shipping.

3. Reliable and Safe: Trains follow dedicated tracks, so they're not affected by road traffic or weather as much as trucks are. This reliability means businesses can count on goods arriving on time and in good condition.

Cargo trains are truly the unsung heroes of transportation, quietly moving essential items while most people are busy focusing on passenger travel.

Special Cars for Special Jobs

Cargo trains are made up of many different types of cars, each designed to carry a specific type of load. Here's a look at some of the unique cars you might see on a cargo train and what they're used to transport.

1. Boxcars: The Generalists

Boxcars are the classic rectangular cars you might picture when you think of a cargo train. They're enclosed, which means they can protect their cargo from weather and damage. Boxcars are versatile and can carry a wide range of goods, including furniture, electronics, clothing, and even canned food.

Fun Fact: Boxcars are one of the oldest types of freight cars, used since the early days of rail transport! They're ideal for items that need to stay safe and dry during the journey.

2. Tank Cars: The Liquid Movers

Some cargo isn't solid, and that's where tank cars come in. Tank cars are long, cylindrical cars specifically designed to carry liquids, such as oil, gasoline, chemicals, and even milk! These cars are built to be leak-proof and have thick walls to handle pressure, ensuring safe transport of their liquid cargo.

Safety First: Because tank cars often carry hazardous materials, they're built with special safety features to prevent leaks or spills, even if the train stops suddenly.

3. Flatcars: The Heavy Lifters

Flatcars are, as the name suggests, flat and open with no sides or roof. They're used for transporting large, heavy items that don't need protection from the weather, like machinery, construction equipment, and even vehicles like cars and trucks. Some flatcars are also equipped with tie-downs to secure their cargo so it doesn't shift during the journey.

Oversized Cargo: Flatcars are perfect for oversized loads that wouldn't fit inside a boxcar, making them essential for transporting large industrial goods.

4. Hopper Cars: The Gravity-Feed Experts

Hopper cars are open-topped cars that transport bulk items, like coal, grain, or sand. They have special chutes at the bottom that allow the contents to be easily unloaded by gravity. When a hopper car reaches its destination, it can be positioned over a grate or pit, and the load simply flows out through the bottom.

Efficiency at Work: Hopper cars make unloading quick and easy, especially for industries like farming and mining, where large quantities of materials need to be moved efficiently.

5. Refrigerated Cars: Keeping It Cool

For items that need to stay cold during transport, there are refrigerated cars, or "reefers." These cars are insulated and equipped with cooling systems to keep their contents fresh. They're commonly used for transporting perishable items like fruits, vegetables, dairy products, and frozen foods.

Keeping Food Fresh: Without refrigerated cars, transporting fresh produce over long distances would be nearly impossible. They're essential for getting food from farms to stores while it's still fresh.

6. Intermodal Cars: Shipping Containers on Rails

Intermodal cars are special because they carry shipping containers—the big, metal boxes you often see on trucks and cargo ships. These cars are part of the intermodal system, which allows containers to be transferred easily between trains, trucks, and ships without unloading their contents. This system makes global trade faster and more efficient.

Global Connections: Intermodal cars allow cargo trains to play a big role in international shipping, helping products travel from one continent to another in a seamless process.

Cargo trains don't just stop at any station like passenger trains do. Instead, they travel between special facilities designed to handle their large loads, called freight terminals. Freight terminals are like train stations for cargo trains, with large cranes, forklifts, and other machinery to load and unload goods.

Here's a look at how cargo trains keep goods moving smoothly from origin to destination:

1. Loading and Unloading at Terminals

When a cargo train arrives at a terminal, it's loaded or unloaded using heavy machinery, depending on the type of goods it's carrying. Shipping containers are lifted by large cranes, while items in boxcars or hopper cars may be moved with forklifts or conveyor belts.

2. Scheduling and Routing

Cargo trains operate on a carefully planned schedule to ensure goods arrive on time. Dispatchers use advanced computer systems to monitor train locations and schedule routes that avoid congestion on the tracks. This precision is essential to keep deliveries reliable and on schedule.

3. Switching and Sorting

Cargo trains often carry cars bound for different destinations. At special switching yards, trains are sorted by destination, and individual cars are grouped with others going to the same location. This "switching" process ensures that goods reach the right place efficiently, even if they're part of a larger train carrying items to multiple destinations.

Fun Facts About Cargo Trains

Longest Freight Train: The longest cargo train ever recorded was over 4 miles long and had over 600 cars! Imagine the power it took to move all that weight!
Cargo Train Speed: While cargo trains aren't as fast as passenger trains, they can reach speeds of up to 60 miles per hour, even with heavy loads.
Environmental Benefits: Trains can move a ton of freight over 470 miles on just one gallon of fuel, making them one of the most eco-friendly ways to transport goods.

Cargo trains may not be as glamorous as passenger trains, but they're a critical part of the transportation system that supports our modern lives. Every time you enjoy fresh fruit, turn on an electronic device, or even drive a car, there's a good chance that some part of it was transported by a cargo train. From food to furniture, cargo trains help bring the world to our doorstep, one journey at a time.

So next time you see a freight train rumbling down the tracks, take a moment to appreciate the incredible role it plays in keeping our world connected. Behind each car is a story of goods moving from factories to stores, farms to cities, and ports to towns—an entire journey that helps keep life moving forward.

13: How Trains Keep Time

Trains aren't just powerful machines that roll down tracks; they're also part of a well-oiled system that relies heavily on timing. Every train follows a schedule, carefully planned and coordinated so passengers can count on arriving at their destinations on time. But how do trains keep to their schedules, and what happens if something causes a delay? In this chapter, we'll explore the world of train timekeeping, how drivers and dispatchers work together to stay on track, and what happens when delays occur.

The Importance of Train Schedules

Train schedules are more than just a list of times at the station —they're the backbone of the entire railway system. Without schedules, trains could easily run into each other, cause traffic jams, or leave passengers stranded. A well-planned schedule ensures that each train has its own "slot" on the tracks and that everything flows smoothly.

Here are a few reasons why train schedules are so essential:

Passenger Convenience: Passengers rely on train schedules to plan their day. Whether they're commuting to work or going on a trip, knowing exactly when the train will arrive is crucial.

Track Sharing: Many trains share the same tracks, so the schedule helps avoid "track traffic." If every train followed its own random timing, it would create chaos on the rails!

Freight Coordination: Passenger and cargo trains often share the same tracks, so the schedule must account for both types of trains, allowing enough time for freight trains to travel without causing delays for passenger trains.

For these reasons, train schedules are carefully crafted to keep the railway system running like clockwork.

Planning the Perfect Schedule

Creating a train schedule is no simple task. Railway companies use computers and skilled planners to create precise timetables for every train. Planners consider the distance between stations, speed limits, time for boarding, and even weather conditions to develop a realistic schedule.

Some factors they consider include:

Travel Time Between Stations: Planners calculate how long it takes for a train to travel from one station to the next, factoring in speed limits, curves, and inclines along the way.

Station Stop Time: They account for how long each train needs to stop at each station. Commuter trains that make frequent stops may only stop for a minute or two, while long-distance trains may need extra time for passengers to board and settle.

Train Type: High-speed trains, local commuter trains, and cargo trains all run at different speeds and have different needs. Planners make sure each train type fits into the schedule without causing congestion.

Once the schedule is finalized, it's distributed to train drivers, dispatchers, and station staff so everyone knows when and where each train should be.

How Train Drivers Follow the Schedule

For a train driver, sticking to the schedule is an essential part of the job. But unlike a car, where you can make up lost time by speeding up, trains must strictly follow speed limits and signals. Here's how drivers keep to the timetable:

1. Keeping an Eye on the Clock

Inside the train cab, the driver has a clock and a copy of the day's timetable. The timetable lists every station, the expected arrival and departure times, and any speed adjustments for specific parts of the journey.

Following the Timetable: Drivers monitor the time carefully, making sure they arrive at each station within a few minutes of the scheduled time. If they're running early, they may need to slow down slightly to avoid arriving before the platform is ready. Adjusting Speed: Drivers can make small adjustments to their speed to stay on schedule. For example, if they're running a bit behind, they might accelerate slightly (within the speed limit) to catch up. However, they must always follow the speed limits and signals for safety.

2. Watching for Signals

Signals play a crucial role in keeping trains on time and in order. Green, yellow, and red signals control when a train can move and when it must stop, helping to space out trains on the track and prevent congestion. So as a reminder from earlier:

Green Light: The track ahead is clear, and the driver can proceed at the scheduled speed.
Yellow Light: Caution! The driver must slow down, as there may be a red signal or another train up ahead.
Red Light: Stop! The track ahead is not clear, and the train must wait for the signal to turn green.

What Happens If There's a Delay?

Delays are an inevitable part of any transportation system, and trains are no exception. Bad weather, technical problems, or even animals on the tracks can cause unexpected delays. Here's how the railway system manages delays to keep everything moving:

1. Communication with Dispatch

The driver stays in constant communication with dispatchers, who monitor all trains on the network from a control center. If the train is delayed, the driver reports the reason to the dispatcher, who can adjust other trains to minimize the impact.

Re-Routing: In some cases, dispatchers might re-route other trains to avoid congestion, especially if a delay is expected to last a while.

Speed Adjustments: If a train is running late but catches up, the dispatcher may instruct the driver to maintain a slightly faster pace (within safe limits) to help recover lost time.

2. Announcements and Passenger Updates

During a delay, the driver or conductor keeps passengers informed by making announcements. Passengers appreciate knowing the reason for the delay and the estimated time of arrival, and regular updates help everyone stay calm.

Clear Communication: Announcements are made clearly over the loudspeaker, often giving details about the cause of the delay (e.g., weather, technical issues) and the expected duration.
Alternative Arrangements: For long delays, train companies may arrange alternative transportation or refund tickets if necessary, ensuring passengers still reach their destinations.

3. Recovery Plans

Once a delay is resolved, drivers and dispatchers work together to bring the train back on schedule. This might involve:

Skipping Stops: In extreme cases, the dispatcher may advise the train to skip certain stops if it's safe and feasible to do so, especially if it helps other trains stay on time.
Speeding Up Within Limits: Drivers may be allowed to increase speed slightly in sections where it's safe, helping to make up for lost time without compromising safety.

14: Weather And Track Conditions

When you think of trains rolling smoothly down tracks, it might seem like they're unstoppable forces that keep going no matter what. But like any other vehicle, trains are affected by the weather! Rain, snow, wind, and even extreme heat can impact tracks and affect how trains operate. Train drivers and railway teams use special techniques and tools to handle these conditions safely and keep journeys as smooth as possible. In this chapter, we'll explore the different ways weather impacts the tracks, how train drivers adapt to changing conditions, and how the railway system stays prepared to handle anything Mother Nature throws its way.

Rain: Slippery Tracks and Slower Speeds

Rain might seem harmless, but wet tracks can make it challenging for trains to stop and accelerate. Here's how rain impacts rail travel and what drivers do to keep trains safe:

The Challenges of Rainy Tracks

Reduced Traction: Just like car tires can slip on wet roads, train wheels can slip on wet rails. Trains rely on the friction between the wheels and rails to grip the track, and rain reduces that grip, making it harder to stop quickly.

Longer Stopping Distances: Because the wheels have less traction on wet rails, trains need more distance to stop. Drivers must start braking earlier than usual, especially as they approach stations and crossings.

Track Wear and Tear: Rainwater can cause tracks to rust and corrode over time, which requires more maintenance. Railway teams work hard to keep the tracks clean and prevent rust from affecting the rails.

Driving Techniques for Rainy Days

On rainy days, train drivers adjust their driving style to account for the slick tracks and reduced visibility:

1. Reduced Speed: Drivers often reduce the train's speed to ensure they have better control and can brake gradually. Slowing down also reduces the risk of skidding.

2. Gentle Acceleration and Braking: Instead of accelerating or braking quickly, drivers use smoother, more gradual motions to avoid sudden jolts or slips.

3. Frequent Communication: Dispatchers and drivers communicate frequently during heavy rain. Dispatchers can provide updates on track conditions, warn about potential flooding, and reroute trains if necessary.

Snow and Ice: The Frozen Challenge

When snow and ice hit the tracks, trains face a new set of challenges. Snow can pile up on the rails, and ice can make the tracks incredibly slippery. These wintry conditions are among the most challenging for trains, but drivers and railway teams have developed strategies to tackle them.

How Snow and Ice Affect Train Tracks

Reduced Traction from Ice: Ice can make tracks even slipperier than rain. A thin layer of ice on the rails can significantly reduce the train's traction, making it harder to stop or even start moving. Snow Accumulation: Snow can pile up on the tracks, especially in heavy storms. If enough snow accumulates, it can obstruct the train wheels or even block the tracks entirely, making travel difficult.

Frost on Electrical Equipment: For electric trains, cold weather can cause frost or ice to form on power lines, reducing the train's ability to receive power and potentially slowing it down.

Snow-Fighting Tools and Techniques

Railways in snowy regions use several tools and techniques to keep trains running smoothly during winter weather:

1. Snowplow Trains: Some trains are equipped with snowplows on the front, which push snow off the tracks as they move. For particularly snowy regions, special snowplow trains are dispatched ahead of passenger trains to clear the tracks.
2. Sand for Traction: Drivers use a clever trick to increase traction on icy rails: sand! Many trains have a small compartment that

dispenses sand onto the tracks in front of the wheels. This sand creates extra grip, helping the train avoid slipping.

3. Heated Tracks: Some tracks have heating systems installed to prevent ice from forming. These systems are typically found in busy urban areas or regions that experience heavy snow. Heated tracks melt ice as it forms, keeping them clear and safe.

Extreme Heat: Warping Tracks and Overheating Engines

While cold weather brings its own set of challenges, extreme heat can also be tough on the railway system. Hot days can affect the rails, trains, and even passengers.

The Impact of Heat on the Rails

Rail Expansion: Metal rails expand when they get hot. If the temperature rises significantly, the rails can expand so much that they start to warp or "buckle." Buckled tracks create bumps and misalignments, which can make it unsafe for trains to pass.

Increased Wear on Equipment: Heat can make engines and other mechanical parts work harder, which can cause wear and tear more quickly than usual. This means extra maintenance is often required in the summer.

Staying Safe in the Heat

Railway teams and drivers take several steps to keep trains running smoothly and safely during hot weather:

1. Reduced Speed on Hot Days: Drivers may be required to slow down when temperatures rise. Slower speeds reduce the risk of derailments on potentially warped tracks and help the train's engine avoid overheating.

2. Extra Inspections: In particularly hot regions, railway maintenance teams check the tracks more frequently, looking for signs of buckling or cracks. They repair any issues quickly to keep the tracks safe.

3. Keeping Passengers Cool: On passenger trains, conductors and crew ensure that air conditioning systems are working properly so passengers stay comfortable in hot weather. If a train's air conditioning fails, passengers may be offered water or alternative transportation to keep them safe.

Fog, Wind, and Other Weather Conditions

While rain, snow, and heat are the biggest weather challenges for trains, fog and high winds can also create unique obstacles.

Fog: Low Visibility and Slow Speeds

Fog reduces visibility, making it hard for drivers to see signals, track markers, or other trains. When driving through fog, train drivers:

Reduce Speed: Slowing down gives the driver more time to react to signals, obstacles, or other trains that might appear suddenly.
Rely on Signals and Communication: With low visibility, drivers rely heavily on signals and frequent communication with dispatchers to stay safe. Dispatchers may provide extra guidance, updating drivers about track conditions and other trains on the line.

High Winds: Blowing Snow, Branches, and Power Lines

High winds can be hazardous for trains, especially in areas with overhead power lines or open, elevated tracks. Strong gusts of wind can cause trees or branches to fall onto the tracks and blow snow or debris onto the rails.

Track Inspections: After a windstorm, track inspectors check for fallen branches, power line issues, or debris that could interfere with trains.
Communication with Dispatch: If the wind is particularly strong, drivers and dispatchers communicate closely to ensure it's safe to proceed. In some cases, trains may slow down or even wait until the winds have calmed to continue.

Whether they're sprinkling sand on icy tracks, clearing snow, or slowing down for fog, the railway team is ready to face every weather challenge with skill, teamwork, and resilience.

15: High-Speed Trains And Bullet Trains

High-speed trains, often called bullet trains, are some of the most exciting and advanced trains in the world. They're built to go faster than regular trains, zipping down tracks at incredible speeds—sometimes faster than a car on the highway or even an airplane during takeoff! These trains have unique designs, specialized tracks, and require highly trained drivers who can handle the speed and precision of driving such powerful machines. In this chapter, we'll take a closer look at high-speed trains, how they work, and the amazing skills it takes to drive one of these lightning-fast trains.

What Makes a High-Speed Train So Fast?

High-speed trains aren't just regular trains going faster. They're designed from the ground up with special features that allow them to reach speeds of up to 200-300 miles per hour! Here's what makes these trains so unique:

1. Aerodynamic Design

High-speed trains are built to be as aerodynamic as possible, meaning they're shaped to cut through the air smoothly with minimal resistance. Bullet trains have a sleek, pointed nose that resembles a bullet (hence the nickname) or even a bird's beak, which helps them move through the air more easily and reduce drag. By minimizing drag, the train can reach higher speeds without needing extra energy.

2. Lightweight Materials

High-speed trains are often made from lightweight yet strong materials like aluminum and carbon fiber, which helps reduce their weight. A lighter train can accelerate more quickly and requires less power to maintain high speeds, making it more efficient. Despite being light, these materials are durable and able to withstand the demands of high-speed travel.

3. Powerful Electric Motors

Unlike traditional trains, which might use diesel engines, most high-speed trains are electric. They're powered by high-voltage electricity from overhead lines or third rails along the track. This electric power allows them to accelerate rapidly, reach high speeds, and maintain a smooth ride for passengers.

4. Advanced Braking Systems

At such high speeds, stopping a train is no easy feat. High-speed trains are equipped with powerful braking systems, including dynamic brakes that use the motors to slow down, and air brakes that create additional friction. Some even use magnetic brakes that create a magnetic field between the train and track, helping the train come to a smooth, quick stop.

Specialized Tracks for High-Speed Trains

High-speed trains can't run on just any railway track. They need specially built tracks designed to handle their speed and prevent any wobbling or derailment. Let's look at some unique features of high-speed rail tracks.

1. Smooth, Straight Tracks

High-speed trains travel best on straight tracks with gentle curves. Tight curves or steep inclines would force the train to slow down, making it difficult to maintain high speeds safely. High-speed rail lines are often laid out over long, straight distances, with any turns designed to be gradual and wide.

2. Elevated Tracks and Tunnels

To avoid obstacles like roads, rivers, or buildings, high-speed tracks often go over or under these obstacles using elevated tracks or tunnels. This design keeps the railway line uninterrupted, allowing the train to travel without having to slow down for crossings or other interruptions.

3. Dedicated Lines

Many high-speed trains run on dedicated lines, meaning that only high-speed trains are allowed on those tracks. This helps avoid traffic from slower trains, which could create delays and safety concerns. In Japan, for example, the Shinkansen, or bullet trains, run on their own network of tracks separate from other trains.

4. Precision Engineering

High-speed rail tracks are meticulously built with extra care to ensure stability. Regular maintenance crews inspect and repair the tracks to keep them perfectly aligned. Even the smallest bump or gap could cause issues for a train moving at hundreds of miles per hour, so the tracks must be kept in top condition at all times.

The Skills Needed to Drive a High-Speed Train

Driving a high-speed train is a job that requires special training, focus, and precision. High-speed train drivers undergo extensive training to learn how to manage the speed, monitor the train's systems, and handle any challenges that might arise.

Popular High-Speed Trains Around the World

High-speed trains are a popular mode of transportation in many countries, known for their speed, comfort, and reliability. Here are some of the most famous high-speed trains around the globe:

Shinkansen (Japan): Known as the original bullet train, the Shinkansen can travel up to 200 mph. It's known for its incredible punctuality, usually arriving within seconds of its scheduled time.
TGV (France): The Train à Grande Vitesse (TGV) in France can reach speeds of around 200 mph. It connects cities like Paris, Lyon, and Marseille, making travel across France fast and convenient.
ICE (Germany): The InterCity Express (ICE) trains in Germany are known for their comfort and speed, reaching up to 186 mph. They connect major German cities and even travel to neighboring countries.
CRH (China): China's high-speed rail network is one of the largest in the world, with trains reaching speeds of up to 217 mph. It connects nearly all major cities in China, making it a popular choice for both short and long-distance travel.
Acela Express (USA): Although slower than other high-speed trains, the Acela Express is the fastest train in the United States, reaching speeds of up to 150 mph on the busy Northeast Corridor between Boston, New York City, and Washington, D.C.

Why High-Speed Trains Matter

High-speed trains offer a fast, efficient alternative to car and plane travel, especially over medium distances. They're also environmentally friendly, using less energy per passenger compared to cars or airplanes, and they reduce road congestion. High-speed rail allows people to travel quickly between cities without the hassle of airport security or traffic jams, making it a popular choice in many countries.

The Future of High-Speed Rail: Going Even Faster!

As technology advances, engineers are working on making high-speed trains even faster. The next generation of high-speed rail includes:

Maglev Trains: These trains use magnetic levitation, meaning they float above the track, eliminating friction. The Shanghai Maglev in China reaches speeds of up to 268 mph, and new maglev trains could reach over 370 mph in the future.

Hyperloop: Though still in development, the Hyperloop concept involves pods that travel through vacuum-sealed tubes, potentially reaching speeds of 600 mph. If successful, it could revolutionize high-speed travel.

High-speed trains are an incredible blend of speed, precision, and technology, allowing passengers to travel vast distances quickly and comfortably. From the careful design of the trains and tracks to the highly trained drivers, everything about high-speed rail is carefully engineered for top performance. Whether it's the iconic Shinkansen in Japan or the TGV in France, high-speed trains bring people and places closer together, offering a thrilling ride and a glimpse into the future of travel.

FAMOUS TRAINS CHECKLIST

Now that you know a lot about trains here is a list of trains you can look for whether out on the rails or in a train museum near you! Have fun!

1. Flying Scotsman – LNER Class A3 4472 (UK)

2. Orient Express – CIWL (Multiple European routes)

3. Shinkansen – Series E5 and E7 (Japan's bullet train)

4. TGV – Train à Grande Vitesse (France)

5. Eurostar – Class 373/374 e320 (UK to Europe)

6. Acela Express – Amtrak Acela (USA)

7. Trans-Siberian Express – Russian Railway (Russia)

8. Rocky Mountaineer – (Canada)

9. Blue Train – (South Africa)

10. ICE – InterCity Express (Germany)

11. Venice Simplon-Orient-Express – (Europe)

12. Hogwarts Express – Jacobite Steam Train, West Coast Railways (Scotland, UK)

13. Glacier Express – Rhaetian Railway (Switzerland)

THE MALLARD

THE FLYING SCOTSMAN

14. Maharajas' Express – (India)

15. Indian Pacific – (Australia)

16. Golden Eagle Trans-Siberian – (Russia)

17. California Zephyr – Amtrak (USA)

18. Rovos Rail – (South Africa)

19. Bernina Express – Rhaetian Railway (Switzerland)

20. Ghan – (Australia)

21. Canadian – VIA Rail Canada (Canada)

22. Shanghai Maglev – (China)

23. XPT – Express Passenger Train (Australia)

24. Jacobite Steam Train – West Coast Railways (Scotland)

25. Belmond Royal Scotsman – (Scotland)

26. Royal Canadian Pacific – (Canada)

27. AVE – Alta Velocidad Española (Spain)

28. Talgo 350 (Renfe Class 102) – (Spain)

29. Thalys – (France, Belgium, Netherlands, Germany)

30. Durango and Silverton Narrow Gauge Railroad – (USA)

31. Nostalgic Rhine Express – (Germany)

32. Tren Crucero – (Ecuador)

33. Eastern & Oriental Express – (Southeast Asia)

34. Palace on Wheels – (India)

35. The Royal Scotsman – (UK)

36. City of New Orleans – Amtrak (USA)

37. ICE 3 – Siemens Velaro (Germany)

38. Zugspitze Railway – (Germany)

39. Nariz del Diablo (Devil's Nose) – (Ecuador)

40. Southwest Chief – Amtrak (USA)

41. Hiawatha – Milwaukee Road (USA)

42. Mallard – LNER Class A4 4468 (UK)

43. Lynton & Barnstaple Railway – (UK)

44. Cass Scenic Railroad – Shay Locomotive (USA)

45. British Pullman – Belmond (UK)

46. Alaska Railroad – Coastal Classic (USA)

47. Sapsan – Velaro RUS (Russia)

48. Settle to Carlisle Line – Class 47 and Class 158 (UK)

49. Bullet Train (Hikari) – Series 0 (Japan)

50. Transalpine – (New Zealand)

This list includes historic trains, luxury trains, high-speed services, and scenic routes, capturing a wide range of famous rail experiences from across the world.

Here is a section to write down the dates and times of trains you have seen!

_____
_____
_____
_____
_____
_____
_____
_____
_____
_____
_____
_____

Made in United States
Troutdale, OR
12/19/2024

26941625R00051